These adventures
belong to:

....

....

....

....

....

First U.S. edition 2018

Library of Congress Catalog Card Number pending
ISBN 978-0-7636-9337-4

GBL 23 22 21 20 19 18
10 9 8 7 6 5 4 3 2 1

Printed in Shenzhen, Guangdong, China

This book was typeset in National Trust TT.
The illustrations were created digitally.

Nosy Crow
an imprint of
Candlewick Press
99 Dover Street
Somerville, Massachusetts 02144

www.nosycrow.com
www.candlewick.com

50

THINGS TO DO
BEFORE YOU'RE

11 $\frac{3}{4}$

nosy crow

An imprint of Candlewick Press

CONTENTS

RANGER

EXPLORER

TRACKER

YOU DID IT!

ACTIVITIES

50 Things to Do Before You're 11 ¾

Welcome to the great outdoors!

Everything you need to have an excellent adventure is in this book! With help from kids all over, we've put together a list of fun challenges — the ultimate 50 things to do before you're 11 ¾. Are you ready? Let's get exploring!

Who's it for?

Whether you're creative and crafty or an active explorer, this book is packed with activities that are fun for everyone! You can do them on your own, with your friends, or with your family. And you don't *have* to be under 11 ¾ — so don't leave the grown-ups behind!

Let's go!

You can do these activities almost anywhere you want: in your backyard, at the park, at the beach, or in the woods!

Note to grown-ups

We recommend that you use your judgment about what is safe and suitable for your children and supervise these activities where necessary. If your little explorers are handling animals, don't forget to put them back where they came from.

Meet the Gang

First things first, there are a few people for you to meet. Say hello to Craig, Rae, and Mia.

CRAIG
Age: 7 ½
Likes: Running, climbing, playing . . . anything outdoors!
Dislikes: Spiders
Favorite activity: Roll Down a Really Big Hill
Explorer type: Active explorer

Map – check!
Compass – check!
Water bottle – check!
That's everything!

These kids have all the know-how you need to complete your 50 things, so keep an eye out for them inside this book. They know lots of cool facts and have some great tips for exploring outdoors!

To find out your explorer type, try our quiz on page 12.

RAE
Age: 11¾
Likes: Photography, tennis, and animals
Dislikes: Singing
Favorite activity: Bring Up a Butterfly
Explorer type: Animal lover

MIA
Age: 11
Likes: Growing her own vegetables and painting
Dislikes: Ketchup
Favorite activity: Plant It, Grow It, Eat It
Explorer type: Creative and crafty

Don't mind my little brother. He can be SO annoying, but he's OK, really! Now, say CHEESE!

Come on, it's time to get going. Adventure, here we come!

Using This Book

Now that you've met the team, let's talk about how to get started on your 50 things. Just get outside and have fun! Easy, right? But don't forget to take this handbook— it's got all the tips you need for an amazing adventure, plus lots of other stuff to do!

Where to start?

You can start at the beginning, or do the activities in any order you like! And if you can't find what you're looking for, just turn to the index on page 94.

When you've completed an activity, write the date and sign your name at the bottom of the page.

Date:
_____

Signature:
_____

Scrapbook

There's notepaper at the back of this book, along with space to stick your photos. That means you can use this as an explorer's journal and fill it with notes, drawings, doodles, memories, and more!

Fun and games

When you're in the car or relaxing at the end of a busy day, check out the quiz and puzzles in the activities section, starting on page 78.

I LOVE taking photos, so my notebook's full of pictures I've taken!

50
11 3/4
An Outdoors Adventure Handbook

What Sort of Explorer Are You?

You're about to start a big adventure. And like all great explorers, you'll discover new places, encounter wild beasts, and travel great distances (well, you'll go on a few long walks). But have you ever wondered what sort of explorer you are? Take this fun quiz and you'll soon find out.

Stay in with a book.

At the front, reading the map. →

It's a rainy day. What do you do?

Grab my boots so I can jump in puddles.

START HERE

You go for a walk with your family. Where are you in the group?

They're great for my art project.

At the back, looking for paw prints — there's a badger den near here! →

You find some feathers on the ground. What do you think?

What bird could they belong to?

12

What's at the top of your backpack?

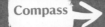

Compass

GADGET WHIZ

You never go out without your gadgets, and you've got the perfect app for everything. You're great to have on a trip and always have the facts at your fingertips. But don't be afraid to jump in and get messy from time to time.

Sketchbook

CREATIVE AND CRAFTY

You love drawing in your sketchbook, making wild art, and gathering materials for your scrapbook. You're always full of fantastic ideas. But that doesn't mean you can't be adventurous at the same time!

Start looking for the perfect shell.

What's the first thing you do when you get to the beach?

ACTIVE EXPLORER

You're always full of energy, and you're the first to try out any new activity – whether it's climbing a tree or rolling down a hill. Don't forget to notice the little details in nature while you're having all that fun!

Take my shoes off and jump right in!

Let's build a raft!

ANIMAL LOVER

You love animals and could watch them for hours! Your quiet, gentle nature means you're good at noticing details in the wild. But don't forget it's fun to be really LOUD and SILLY sometimes, too!

ou come to a ream on your lk. What's your irst thought?

Let's look for frog spawn!

13

Get Ready

This handbook's all about YOU. It's your place to write ideas, draw what you see, and stick in leaves, tickets, photos, or anything else! Now it's time to start recording your own adventures.

First, fill in this passport with all your explorer details. Find an old photo to stick in or, if you're feeling creative, you could draw a self-portrait instead.

EXPLORER PASSPORT

NAME:

....

DATE OF BIRTH:

....

HEIGHT:

....

EYE COLOR:

....

PHOTOGRAPH OR PICTURE

Explorer's checklist

All explorers need supplies, so here are a few ideas for when you're packing. You won't need all these things at once, but the essentials are handy for whatever adventure you're having!

The essentials:
- ☐ Walking shoes or sneakers
- ☐ Water bottle
- ☐ Warm clothes
- ☐ Raincoat

And the rest:
- ☐ Notebook
- ☐ Pencil
- ☐ Sunblock
- ☐ Map
- ☐ Compass
- ☐ Binoculars
- ☐ Net (for catching fish or bugs)
- ☐ Bucket
- ☐ String
- ☐ Flashlight
- ☐ Swimsuit and towel
- ☐ Camera

Top tip!

Remember to think about the weather and what activity you're planning. It will be a wet drive home if you forget to pack a towel for your beach trip!

15

Mapping

Having a map is useful when you're an explorer. After all, you always need to find your way around. Here's a space to draw a map of your very own!

Draw on it, write on it, and use it as a record of all your adventures. We even have a few ideas to get you started.

Make your mark!

- Draw a map of your town or state
- Draw a house or make a big dot to show where you live.
- As you go, mark the places where you've done your 50 things.
- If you go on a road trip, draw the route you took.

Who knows where you might go to do your 50 things? But with this map, you can keep track of everywhere you've been!

Explorer Tips and Hints

You're nearly ready to get started, but before you head out the door, Craig and Rae have some top explorer tips and hints.

Handy hints for watching wildlife

- If you want to see wild animals, remember to be VERY still and quiet, and don't wear anything too brightly colored.
- Many animals will never come very close to humans. You'll have a better chance of seeing them if you use binoculars.
- Dogs will scare wild animals away even if they're well behaved, so leave your pets at home.
- Never feed wild animals. You might accidentally give them something they shouldn't eat.

Rae's top tip!

Try sitting in one spot for fifteen minutes and writing down all the wildlife you see. You could be surprised!

Make sure you stay safe and look after wildlife. If in doubt, follow these simple rules!

The Countryside Code

1. Stay safe – plan your trip ahead.
2. Leave gates as you find them and follow local signs.
3. Always take your trash home.
4. Stay on the path – don't walk through crops.
5. Don't go near farm animals or machinery.
6. Keep a safe distance from wild animals.
7. If your family has a dog, keep it under control.
8. Don't disturb other people.

Craig's top tip!

Get your friends to join in too! See who can make the biggest mud pie, fly their kite the longest, or catch the biggest crab!

ADVENTURER

These ten activities should be at the top of everyone's list! They're sure to give you a taste for ADVENTURE!

Top tip!

Don't forget to take photos as you go. You can stick them in this book to remember your adventures!

1 Climb a Tree

Do you know what type of tree you climbed?

See if its leaves match any of these:

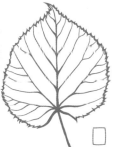

☐ BIRCH

☐ SYCAMORE

☐ OAK

If not, draw your leaf here.

Date:

_____

Signature:

_____

Once you've climbed a tree, fill in the date to show you've completed this activity!

Remember that trees can be slippery if it's rained recently. It's a good idea to check before you climb.

Roll Down a Really Big Hill

It's the fun way to get to the bottom!

3 Camp Out in the Wild

Why sleep in a boring bed when you can sleep outside under the stars?

Date:

_____

Signature:

_____

What natur
sounds did
you hear?

Did they
sound like
any of these
animals?

What noise did you make rolling down the hill? Draw what you looked like when you got to the bottom!

First check that there are no steep drops or anything in the way (especially if it's brown and smelly) and off you go!

Date:

_____

Signature:

_____

 □ OWL

 □ FOX

□ DEER

□ FROG

 □ OGRE

 □ YOUR FRIEND SNORING!

Did you know?

Being in a tent might mean you hear the dawn chorus, when songbirds sing at the start of a new day.

23

4 Build a Fort

Branches, twigs, and leaves make surprisingly cozy forts.

5 Skip a Stone

Can you get four bounces?

What type of skip did you do?

The Missile

The Stealth

The Bouncer

Stick your favorite
fort photo in here! ←

Date:

_____

Signature:

_____

Top tip!

Can't get your fort to
stand up? If you lean it
against a tree, it should
stay up more easily.

Did you know?

As your old fort rots, it
will be eaten by fungi,
insects, and other creepy
crawlies — all of which
love rotting wood.

Top tip!

The best place to
skip a stone is
somewhere with
flat water where
there's a safe place
to stand.

Date:

_____

Signature:

_____

Did you know?

Slate rocks are the best
for skipping, and the
smoother, rounder,
and flatter the better!
Get low to the ground
and throw your stone
hard so it skims across
the top of the water.

25

Run Around in the Rain

Time to make a splash!

After you're done splashing in puddles, make a footprint on a piece of paper. Wait for it to dry, then cut it out and stick it here!

Date:

_____

Signature:

_____

Fly a Kite

Windy days are perfect for flying kites.
Design your own kite in the space below.

For your kite to fly, it needs a nice clear sky, windy weather, and a large, open space. Look out for trees, houses, and power lines!

Date:

_____

Signature:

_____

8 Catch a Fish with a Net

You have to be quick to catch a fish!

What kind of fish did you see?
Do they match any of these?

☐ TROUT

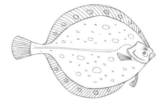
☐ FLOUNDER

☐ STICKLEBACK

☐ EEL

Don't forget to set
your fish free after
you've carefully
taken a look at it!

Tell us more about
the fish you caught.

Which one is your favorite?

....

How big is it?

....

What's its favorite food?

....

What's the best thing about it?

....

**Can you draw your
favorite fish here?**

Date:

_____

Signature:

_____

Eat an Apple Straight from a Tree

9

I love apples!

Can you stick the seeds from the apple you picked onto the page? Maybe you can feed the caterpillar.

Did you know?

There are more than 7,000 different types of apples in the world. What's the name of the one you picked?

Date:

Signature:

Fall Fun!

Visit a pumpkin patch and pick out one to carve. With a grown-up's help, draw a face and cut it into the orange gourd.

Date:

_____

Signature:

_____

10

Pick a Pumpkin

DISCOVERER

Do you like getting a bit messy? Are you brave enough to pick up a snail? Then these activities are for you! It's time to start DISCOVERING!

Top tip!

Sometimes it's great to get really messy. But don't forget to wash your hands afterward!

11 Go on a Really Long Bike Ride

The speedy way to explore the great outdoors!

Date:
_____

Signature:
_____

Top tips for biking

Follow the rules of the road and don't forget to wear a helmet!

Show us how muddy you got!

Cycle over a piece of paper, then stick it here to show your tire mark!

12 Make a Trail with Sticks

Use sticks as arrows to mark a path through the woods.

Top tip!

Turn it into a treasure hunt by bringing something to hide at the end.

Date:

_____

Signature:

_____

13 Make a Mud Pie

Recipe: Mud. More mud.

Date:

_____

Signature:

_____

What sort of mud pie are you going to make? Draw it on this plate.

Top tip!
Every good pie needs some decorations. Stones, sticks, shells, and leaves all make great mud-pie toppings.

Dam a Stream

It won't be long before the stream's a pond!

How high is your dam?

Once you've managed to make your pond, use the ruler on page 74 to see how high your dam is.

Date:

_____

Signature:

_____

Top tip!

After you've had your fun, remove the dam. Lots of creatures may be depending on that stream for their habitat.

Play in the Snow

15

Keep your fingers cozy and your feet toasty.

Snowy ideas!
Check off the things you've done!

☐ Build a snowman
☐ Erect a snow fort
☐ Make a snow angel
☐ Throw snowballs

Date:

_____

Signature:

_____

Did you know?

Snow is made from lots of tiny ice crystals, known as snowflakes. No two flakes are exactly the same.

Make a Daisy Chain

Perfect for summer days!

Stick your daisy chain here.

Set up a Snail Race

17

On your marks, get set, go . . . slowly.

Give the snails some racing colors!

Color in the snails below to create your racing colors.

Date:

_____

Signature:

_____

Did you know?

Picking daisies encourages future growth!

Top tip!

Try to find daisies with long, thick stems to make your chain. They will be easier to make holes in and less likely to break apart.

Did you know?

If you keep your snail cool and moist, it will have the best chance of winning. Don't forget to put your snails back where you found them once they've finished racing.

Date:

_____

Signature:

_____

Top tip!

Use tasty-looking leaves to tempt your snail to move faster toward the finish line.

18 Create Wild Art

Use leaves, sticks, pinecones, or anything you like to create a work of art!

Exhibit your art in this frame!

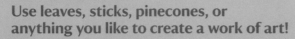

Title of masterpiece:

Date:

Signature:

Play Poohsticks

19

The best bridges for poohsticks are traffic-free.

Top tip!

Decorate your stick by tying a leaf or some grass to it. You'll know exactly which one is yours when it comes out the other side of the bridge,

Who won?

1st:

2nd:

3rd:

Date:

Signature:

20 # Jump Over Waves

Big, small, blue, or green – all waves are great to jump over!

Try these jumps out!

THE SUPERHERO

THE GIANT LEAP

Date:

Signature:

THE NINJA

Pick a spot where you know the depth of the water so you don't jump in where it's too deep!

41

RANGER

Are you ready to explore a bit farther afield? Then grab your backpack and get out there, RANGER!

Pick Wild Blackberries

They're not just tasty treats—
they make great drawing tools too!

Color in the blackberry.
Blackberry juice makes
great paint.

Did you know?
The blackberry farthest
along the branch, away
from the center of the
blackberry bush, is
the tastiest!

Date:

_____

Signature:

_____

Explore Inside a Tree

Date:

_____

Signature:

_____

Some trees have hollows so big you can climb right inside!

Did you know?

Lots of insects, such as beetles, live inside hollow trees and eat the rotting wood. Look closely and you'll see their burrowing holes.

Make a bark rubbing

Place a piece of paper on a tree and rub over it with crayons to see what happens. Then stick your bark rubbing in this space!

23
Visit a Farm

One of the best places to make new furry friends.

Make this page look like a farm!
Collect as many things as you can, like straw, feathers, wool, or whatever you like, and stick them on the page.

Can you match the farm animals to the footprints?

GOOSE

CHICKEN

HORSE

PIG

COW

Date:

_____

Signature:

_____

After your farm visit, it's best to wash your hands clean of germs before eating or drinking.

45

Go on a Walk Barefoot

24

You'll never want to put your shoes back on once you feel the tickly grass between your toes.

Stand here and trace around your toes!

Date:

_____

Signature:

_____

Keep your eyes peeled for glass or other things that might poke you.

Date:

_____

Signature:

_____

25

Make a Grass Trumpet

Blow into a blade of grass and start up the band!

Stick your grass trumpet here.

Stick here

How to make the best trumpet:

1. Pick your perfect piece of grass. Look for a long straight piece that's thick and dry.

2. Put your thumbs together and hold the blade of grass between them, gripping the grass with the top and bottom of your thumbs.

3. Take the biggest breath you can and blow between your thumbs. As the air flows over the grass, you should hear a whistling sound.

4. If you don't hear anything, move the blade of grass a little and try again.

26 Hunt for Fossils and Bones

27 Go Stargazing

Top tip!

Stargazing is best done before the moon is full, so it might be worth looking at the next new moon dates before you plan your stargazing evening.

Date:

_____

Signature:

_____

Can you conn the stars to create the constellation See if you can spot them in t night sky.

Make sure you know the Fossil Code:

1. Stay away from cliffs and cliff edges.
2. Always go collecting when the tide is going out.
3. Be aware of weather conditions.
4. Collect only things that have been naturally unearthed or washed up.
5. Take a grown-up with you.

Date:

_____

Signature:

_____

CASSIOPEIA

ORION

Don't forget Orion's sword!

THE BIG DIPPER

Can you spot the North Star?
Once you've found the Big Dipper, follow the two stars at the front of it upward and you will find the North Star. This star was used by navigators to sail around the world because it showed them which way was north.

49

Keep an eye out for drops and edges!

Date:

_____

Signature:

_____

28

Climb a Huge Hill

Go to the top and touch the sky!

Date:

_____

Signature:

_____

29

Explore a Cave

Don't forget your flashlight – you're going to need it!

Make a noise and listen for its echo. What did it sound like?

Top tip!

Bring an adult with you and follow good caving practice. Even experts never enter a cave alone!

Hold a Scary Beast

30

It might be scary at the time, but think how brave you'll feel after!

What creature were you brave enough to hold?
Can you draw a picture of it?

There are loads of amazing scary beasts out there, like slimy slugs and big beetles. Avoid wasps, bees, and brown furry caterpillars as they might bite or sting.

Date:

_____

Signature:

_____

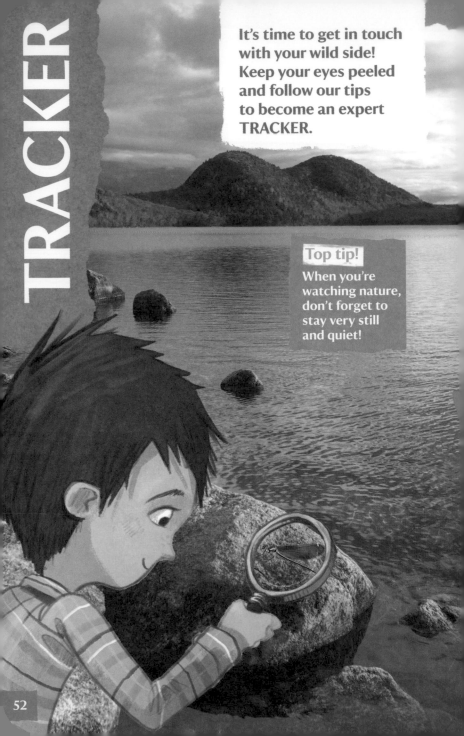

TRACKER

It's time to get in touch with your wild side! Keep your eyes peeled and follow our tips to become an expert TRACKER.

Top tip!

When you're watching nature, don't forget to stay very still and quiet!

1

Date:
_____

Signature:
_____

Hunt for Bugs

What's the creepiest crawly you can find?

Did you know?
Insects make up about 80 percent of the world's species.

What creepy-crawly did you catch?
Can you draw it?

32 Find Frog Spawn

Just wait until the tadpoles hatch!

Date:
_____

Signature:
_____

Did you know?
Frog spawn looks like a thick jelly laid in clumps. Toad spawn looks similar but is laid in long chains.

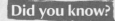

53

34 Track Wild Animals

33 Catch a Falling Leaf

It's harder than you think!

Stick the leaves you caught here.

Top three tracking tips:

35 Discover What's in a Pond

Date:

_____

Signature:

_____

Pond water is full of life. Scoop some into a tub and check out what's living in it!

Animals are easy to find if you follow their footprints, feathers, fur, and poop.

Date:

_____

Signature:

_____

1. Examine a footprint. How big is it? How many toes are there?

2. Look at the pattern of the track. Figure out how it moves.

3. Look for other signs. Do you think the animal has a tail?

What did you find?
Draw anything you spot below.

Top tip!

Scoop the net three times in a figure eight to pick up the littlest creatures, then empty the contents into a tub of pond (not tap!) water. If you don't spot anything at first, take a closer look.

Date:

_____

Signature:

_____

Remember to return your new friends to their homes!

Make a Home for a Wild Animal

36

It's not just dogs, cats, hamsters, and fish that need homes!

Take a photo of your wild house and stick it here.

Date:

_____

Signature:

_____

How to!

You could make an insect hotel, a squirrel home, or even a nesting box for birds. You can make an easy insect hotel just by placing sticks or plant stems in an empty plastic bottle.

37

Check Out the Curious Creatures in a Tide Pool

What's the most amazing thing you can find?

Tell us more about the creature you saw . . .

What was it?

....

What color was it?

....

How big was it?

....

Draw one of the creatures you saw in the circle above.

Date:

_____

Signature:

_____

Did you know?

Sea stars can push their stomachs out of their mouths so they can gobble up and digest anything that's too big to swallow.

Bring Up a Butterfly

38

Take a caterpillar home with you and watch it turn into a beautiful butterfly. Then set it free and watch it fly away!

What you need to get started:

1. A caterpillar
2. A large plastic tub with small holes in the lid
3. Leaves from the plant where you found your caterpillar
4. Slightly damp soil to line the bottom of the tub
5. A twig or two to lean against the side of the tub

Keep a short diary!

Write down how your caterpillar changes at the end of each week.

Week 1

Week 2

Week 3

Week 4

Week 5

Week 6

Bring the butterflies to life!

Make them as colorful as you can and give them names.

Name:

Name:

Top tip!

Avoid hairy caterpillars as some can sting. Monarchs, painted ladies, and queen butterflies are a few good options.

Date:

Signature:

59

Catch a Crab

Top tip!

Scraps of bacon and fish make really good crab bait.

Go on a Nature Walk at Night

Date:

_____

Signature:

_____

Can you connect the dots to finish this crab?

Draw in its feet and claws to help it reach the bait!

How to:

Tie a stone and bait to the end of some string so that it sinks. When you feel the string tugging, pull it up at a steady pace – too quickly and the crab will fall off, too slowly and it will eat the bait. Be very careful when you pick crabs up (they're not afraid to use those pincers), and don't forget to put them back in the water afterward.

Try switching off your flashlight for ten minutes. Can you see in the dark or hear any animals?

Top tip!

Plan your walk for a full moon so you can see where you're going!

Take a grown-up with you.

EXPLORER

Are you ready for a challenge? These adventurous activities are ones you won't forget in a hurry! Let's go EXPLORING!

Top tip!

These aren't all things you'd try every day. Plan ahead so that you have time to prepare and look forward to your expedition.

Plant It, Grow It, Eat It

41

Just like you, fruit and vegetables need time to grow, but they're definitely worth the wait!

How's it growing?

Draw a picture and measure your plant's height to show how well it's been growing.

Week 1:

....

Week 2:

....

Week 3:

....

Date:

_____

Signature:

_____

Top tip!

Old rain boots and even jam jars make great places to grow your plants. Just add soil!

Go Swimming in the Ocean

42

Bounce over waves while practicing your backstroke.

Don't forget to take your swimming goggles!

Build a Raft

43

Take to the water in your homemade raft. But be prepared for it to sink!

How to:

1. First you need something to make your raft float. Look for empty barrels or collect used drink bottles. Anything full of air will do.
2. Next, make the body of your raft. Most rafts have a basic wooden frame.
3. Tie your floats together and attach them to the raft's body.
4. If your raft is big enough to carry you, don't forget to wear a life jacket!

Date:

_____

Signature:

_____

Top tip!

To stay safe, only swim on beaches with lifeguards, and always follow their signs and instructions.

The ocean can be powerful, so make sure you have a grown-up with you, and only swim where the water is calm.

Date:

_____

Signature:

_____

Attach a photo of your raft.

If you don't want to get wet, make a mini raft by tying some twigs together with long pieces of grass or straw. Attach a leaf for a sail and set your raft on the water!

Top tip!

With a grown-up, launch your raft from a calm section of water.

65

44

Go Bird-Watching

Be as quiet as a mouse and watch the birds at play.

Don't forget your binoculars!

What types of birds did you spot?

Do they match any of the drawings below?

☐ PIGEON

Look out for robins' red tummies →

☐ ROBIN

Or draw your bird here:
↓

☐ SEAGULL

Date:

_____

Signature:

_____

Did you know?

There are more than 10,000 different types of birds in the world.

5

Navigate Using a Map and Compass

You'll never get lost if you can use these trusty tools.

Draw your own map of where you went and what you saw here.

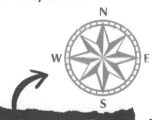

Did you know?

This shape, called a compass rose, is often found on maps and compasses. The different points on the rose indicate where north, east, south, and west are.

Date:

_____

Signature:

_____

Try Rock Climbing

Keep your eyes peeled for some big cracks and places to get a good grip.

☐ The sky

Top tip!

Only climb in a safe, supervised setting and remember to ALWAYS wear a helmet when you are rock climbing.

Look for nearby rock climbing gyms or indoor rock walls to get some practice.

☐ Empire State Building

☐ A tree

Date:

_____

Signature:

_____

☐ A car

Did you know?

The youngest person to climb Mount Everest so far was only thirteen!

How high did you climb?

Cook on a Campfire

There's no kitchen in the great outdoors, but you don't have to miss dinner!

Draw your very own campfire meal in the pan!

Top tip!

Baked potatoes are great camping food. Potatoes can easily be wrapped in foil and cooked in a fire. Serve them up with some baked beans!

Date:

_____

Signature:

_____

48

Ride a Horse

Soon you'll be riding like a proper jockey!

Design your own racing colors.

What was your horse's name?

Name:

Date:
_____

Signature:
_____

Find a Geocache

For all those who love a treasure hunt outdoors!

What is it?

A geocache is a little treasure box hidden outside. All you need to find it is a handheld GPS device! For events near you and more details, look up a geocaching website.

What did you find in your geocache?

And what did you put in it for others to find?

Date:

Signature:

Did you know?

The first recorded geocache was in Oregon in 2000.

71

Research an outdoor activity center near you—you may be able to rent a canoe or take a class.

Canoe Down a River

50

See the world from a duck's point of view.

☐ DRAGONFLY

☐ MUSKRAT

☐ SWAN

What did you see by the riverside?

Date:

_____

Signature:

_____

☐ BEAVER

Top tips!

1. Be sure you can swim at least fifty meters (the length of an Olympic-sized pool).

2. Make sure you've got the right equipment, especially a life jacket.

3. Check the weather forecast before you hea out on the water.

4. Check the navigation and events happening o your route.

5. Bring an expert with yo

You Did It!

Well done! You completed all 50 things! So how was it? We hope you had a fantastic adventure!

Now that you're done, don't let those memories fade. Use the next few pages to record all your very best memories. Then try your hand at some of these puzzles!

Wondering why there's a ruler here? Turn the page to find out.

cm
mm 1   2   3
inches 1/8   1   2   3   4   5   6   7   8   9   10   11   12   13   14   15   16   17   18   19
1   2   3   4   5   6   7

Ruler

Some of the activities in this book require a ruler. If you don't have one with you, just cut along the dotted line and use the ruler on this page.

You might be surprised at how small – or how BIG! – some animals are. Write down any measurements you take on this page.

Top fact!

Did you know that the pygmy shrew is one of the smallest mammals in the world at only 7 cm long?

pygmy shrew – 7 cm

millipede – 6 cm

acorn – 3 cm

bee – 1 cm

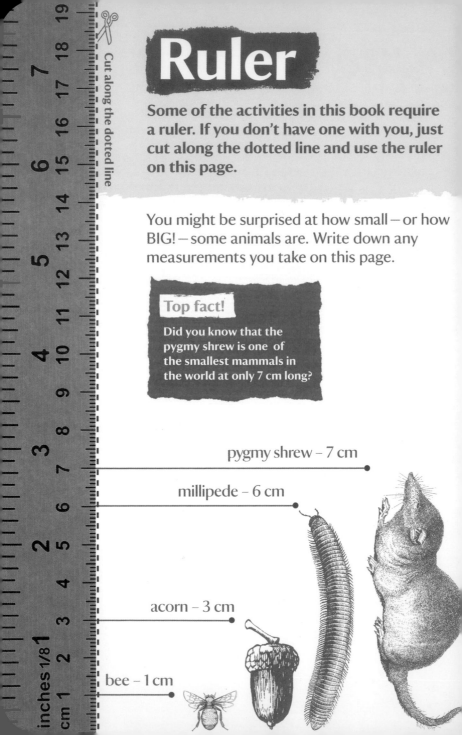

My Favorites

What did you think of the activities? What was the messiest? The scariest?

Fill in this chart with the messiest, noisiest, and silliest things you've tried!

	Which activity	Why I liked it
Messiest		
Noisiest		
Scariest		
Most beautiful		
Most exciting		
Most difficult		
Best with friends		
Best with animals		
Best at night		
Best in summer		
Best in winter		

Add some more ideas here!

The Winner Is . .

So what was your absolute FAVORITE activity? Well, we think it deserves a prize for being so great, don't you?

Fill in this page to make it all about your personal No. 1!

1st

Doodle in lots more decoration.

Color the ribbon in your favorite color.

Complete the details on the trophy.

Number 1 activity:

....

Date awarded:

....

Completed by (name):

....

Other things to try

Can you think of 10 more things you want to do before you're 11¾? They could be anything from surfing to archery. List them here:

1 ....

2 ....

3 ....

4 ....

5 ....

6 ....

7 ....

8 ....

9 ....

10 ....

Doodle Time

Whether you're on a long car journey, lounging on the beach, or chilling in the park, these activities are just what you need to keep busy. So grab a pen or pencil and get to it!

Color in Rae's umbrella.

Add more splashes to this puddle.

Fill the branches with birds or leaves.

You could even draw a rainbow in the sky!

Complete the flowers!

Who do you think lives in this hollow?

Fill in the Blanks!

Dot to dot

Something's been left behind in the grass. But what is it?

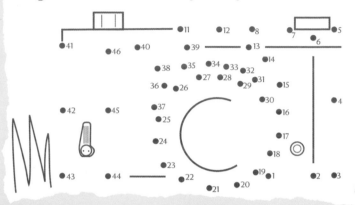

Picture perfect

Can you copy this picture of Craig? It's not as hard as it sounds! Just use the grid and copy one square at a time.

Fill in the missing words to make up your own story. You can use whatever words and names you want!

THE NEWS

FAMOUS EXPLORER MAKES GREAT DISCOVERY!

Today, world-famous explorer

_____ has made a

fantastic discovery! While trekking

across _____,

the explorer's team saw a strange

_____ and decided to

follow it. This led them to an

enormous _____.

Speaking about their find,

the expedition leader, _____,

said, "I've been exploring the great

PHOTOGRAPH OR DRAWING

outdoors since I was _____ years old,

and I never thought I'd see anything like this _____.

It's definitely the _____ I've ever seen!

It's been a _____ expedition, but none of it would have

been possible without the help of my _____ and _____."

This discovery will make _____ one of the most famous

_____ in the _____!

Puzzles

Once you've finished the puzzles, you can check th answers on page 87!

Word Search

Can you find the names of fifteen animals hidden in the grid? They could be vertical, horizontal, diagonal, or backward!

Y	D	R	I	B	K	C	A	L	B
L	Z	F	S	R	A	S	M	A	A
F	T	I	B	B	A	R	D	M	T
R	D	S	W	P	J	G	C	O	P
E	O	H	O	F	E	Y	I	U	N
T	L	E	R	R	I	U	Q	S	H
T	P	Y	M	O	B	R	X	E	B
U	H	E	D	G	E	H	O	G	D
B	I	W	S	E	G	K	N	T	F
O	N	R	D	P	E	E	H	S	Z

Badger
Bat
Blackbird
Butterfly
Crab
Deer
Dolphin
Fish
Frog
Hedgehog
Mouse
Rabbit
Sheep
Squirrel
Worm

Sudoku

Finish this grid so that each row, column, and block of four squares contains a kite, a flower, a fish, and a star.

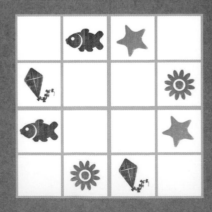

82

Crossword

Solve the clues to fill in the missing nature words!

Across
1. Squirrels gather these
2. A baby butterfly
5. Birds make one in spring
6. A bird with a red chest

Down
1. The best time of year for picking pumpkins
2. A rock pool creature with big pincers
3. A cluster of frogs' eggs
4. Where you sleep when you go camping

Word Scramble

Unscramble these words to find seven items you might pack in your backpack. (For clues, turn to page 15.)

tware _ _ _ _ _

remaca _ _ _ _ _ _

pma _ _ _

sampocs _ _ _ _ _ _ _

ten _ _ _

thilghalfs _ _ _ _ _ _ _ _ _

bulkscon _ _ _ _ _ _ _ _

Maze

84

EXIT

Quick-Fire Quiz

Did you know that there are world records for many of the activities in this book?

Test your knowledge or try these questions on your friends! The answers are on page 8?

1) How big is the largest kite ever?
  a) 83 feet across
  b) 16 feet across
  c) 350 feet across

2) What is the record for skips of a stone on water?
  a) 12
  b) 88
  c) 204

3) What is the world record for the biggest pumpkin ever grown?
  a) 1,200 pounds
  b) 5,000 pounds
  c) 2,624 pounds

4) When was the first compass invented?
  a) Around 1400 CE
  b) Around 100 CE
  c) Around 300 BCE

5) What is the world record for miles cycled in one year?
  a) 75,065 miles (three times around the world)
  b) 904 miles
  c) 150,256 miles

6) What is the greatest height ever rock-climbed in one day?
  a) half a mile
  b) 500 feet
  c) 5.4 miles

7) The snail-racing championships take place in England every year. What is the record time for a snail to complete the 33-centimeter course?
  a) 23 seconds
  b) 2 minutes
  c) 20 minutes

8) How old is the oldest known tree in the U.S.?
  a) 400 years old
  b) 150 years old
  c) At least 4,000 years old

9) What is the longest solo journey made in a canoe?
  a) 150,057 miles
  b) 90 miles
  c) 2,010 miles

10) How large is the biggest species of crab in the world?
  a) 12 feet
  b) 8 inches
  c) 30 feet

Answers

So how did you do?
Check your answers here!

Word Search

```
Y D R I B K C A L B
I Z F S R A S M A A
F T I B B A R D M T
R D S W P J G C O P
E O H O F E Y I U N
T L E R R I U Q S H
T P Y M O B R X E B
U H E D G E H O G D
B I W S E G K N T F
O N R D P E E H S Z
```

Crossword

```
          ¹A C O R N S        ³
          U                   F
²C A T E R P I L L A R        R
 R        U                   O
 A        M      ⁴            G
 B     ⁵N E S T               S
                 E            P
                 N            A
                 T            W
              ⁶R O B I N
```

Word Scramble

1. Water, 2. Camera,
3. Map, 4. Compass,
5. Net, 6. Flashlight,
7. Sunblock

Maze

Quick-Fire Quiz

1. a; 2. b; 3. c; 4. c;
5. a; 6. c; 7. b; 8. c;
9. c; 10. a

Picture Gallery

Stick your photos here or doodle in the frames.

Notepaper

Use these pages to jot things down while you're out and about!

Index

Image Credits

p. 1: © Kritchanut; p. 6: © Andrew Burgess/Shutterstock (bottom right); © Maryna S/Shutterstock (bottom left); © Prapann/Shutterstock (bottom); p. 7: © Zepedrocoelho/Shutterstock; pp. 8–9: © Jiraphoto/Shutterstock; p. 10: © suns07butterfly/Shutterstock; p. 11: © rzarek/Shutterstock; p. 12: © JGade/Shutterstock; p. 13: © Tribalium/Shutterstock (center right); © pixelprohd/Shutterstock (top left); © istockpLisa Thornberg (left); p. 15: © jukurae/Shutterstock (right); © Rost9/Shutterstock (bottom left); © Bildagentur Zoonar GmbH/ Shutterstock (bottom center); © Marynka/Shutterstock (top right); p. 16: © bsd/Shutterstock (top right); © elegeyda/Shutterstock (bottom); p. 17: © Jamie Farrant/Shutterstock (center); © Elena Kazanskaya/Shutterstock (bottom); pp. 18–19: © chrupka/Shutterstock (center); © Ian 2010/Shutterstock (bottom); © napas chalermch Shutterstock (bottom left); p. 20: © Dudarev Mikhail/ Shutterstock; p. 21: © Miro art studio/Shutterstock; p. 22: © Kokhanchikov/Shutterstock (bottom left); pp. 22–23: © Jiraphoto/Shutterstock; p. 23: © thumbelina/ Shutterstock (center); © Vasilyeva Larisa/Shutterstock (far left); © La puma/Shutterstock (left); © Dean Murray/Shutterstock (bottom left); © moopsi/Shutterstock (right); © Ilya Zonov/Shutterstock (far left); © Katunina/Shutterstock (bottom right) p. 24: © gdvcom/Shutterstock (top left); © bawan/Shutterstock (top left); © NRT/Shutterstock; © elegeyda/Shutterstock (bottom); p. 25: © Natalia Sheinkin/Shutterstock (top left); © NRT/Shutterstock; p. 26: © almgren/Shutterstock; p. 27: © winnond/Shutterstock; © Annette Shaff/ Shutterstock (top, bottom); p. 28: © National Trust/Rob Salter (bottom left); p. 28: © Lemonade Serenade/ Shutterstock (center left); © fire_fly/Shutterstock (center right); © Sabelskaya (bottom); pp. 28–29: © Anthonycz/Shutterstock; p. 29: © Tribalium/Shutterstock; p. 30: © Vector/Shutterstock (top); © raysay/ Shutterstock (bottom); p. 31: © Jacek Fulawka/Shutterstock (centre); p. 32: © Karen Grigoryan/Shutterstock; p. 33: © greenland/Shutterstock (center); © Jason Winter/Shutterstock (right); © thumbelina/Shutterstock (center); p. 34: © graphixmania/Shutterstock (center); © Strejman/Shutterstock; © diogoppr/Shutterstock; p. 35: © diogoppr/Shutterstock; © Strejman/Shutterstock; © Andrey_Kuzmin/Shutterstock (bottom); p. 36: © Festa/Shutterstock; © graphixmania/Shutterstock; p. 37: © Max Topchii/Shutterstock; p. 38: © chrisbrignell/ Shutterstock; p. 39: © chrisbrignell/Shutterstock (center); © pio3/Shutterstock (bottom); p. 40: © National Trust Images; p. 41: © Leremy/Shutterstock (bottom right); © graphixmania/Shutterstock (top right); p. 42: © winnond/Shutterstock (top); © ollirg/Shutterstock; p. 43: © Anna Kucherova/Shutterstock (center, top right) © Linda Vostrovska/Shutterstock; p. 44: © Conny Sjostrom/Shutterstock; p. 45: © Nouwens/Shutterstock (top center); © Helga Chirk/Shutterstock (bottom left); p. 46: © TravnikovStudio/Shutterstock (bottom right); p. 47: © julie deshaies/Shutterstock (center); © Lina Valunaite/Shutterstock (bottom); p. 48: © MIGUEL GARCIA SAAVEDRA/Shutterstock (top right); © IhorZigor/Shutterstock (center right); © Prapann/Shutterstock; p. 49 © Janos Levente/Shutterstock; p. 50: © IR Stone/Shutterstock; p. 51: © Vitalii Hulai Shutterstock (left); © Eric Isselee/Shutterstock (bottom left); © Jiraphoto/Shutterstock; p. 52: © JaysonPhotography/Shutterstock; © Dmitriy Kurnyavko/Shutterstock (bottom); p. 53: © Dmitriy Kurnyavko/Shutterstock (top); © BMJ/Shutterstock (bottom); p. 54: © Fotofermer/Shutterstock; © Chros/Shutterstock (bottom right); p. 55: © sarininka/ Shutterstock (bottom right); © Helga Chirk/Shutterstock (top); p. 56: © THPStock/Shutterstock; p. 57: © Peter Mukherjee; (center, top right) © thumbelina/Shutterstock; p. 58: © istockpLisa Thornberg; © Vector/ Shutterstock (center right); p. 59: © Stepan_Bormotov; p. 60: © A7880S/Shutterstock; p. 61: © Nuttapong/ Shutterstock; © Prapann/Shutterstock; p. 62: © Helen Hotson/Shutterstock; p. 64: © s_oleg/Shutterstock (top); © Great_Kit/Shutterstock (center left) © Ramona Heim/Shutterstock (bottom right); p. 65: © dghagi (bottom); © Anthonycz/Shutterstock (left); p. 66: © chronicler/Shutterstock (left); © aggressor/Shutterstock (right); © Fotonium/Shutterstock (bottom left); © Nouwens/Shutterstock (center); p. 67: © Morphart Creation Shutterstock (center right); © sergign/Shutterstock (top right); p. 69: © AkeSak Shutterstock (bottom center) © Jiraphoto/Shutterstock (bottom); © graphixmania/Shutterstock (bottom); p. 70: © Rashad Ashurov/ Shutterstock (top right); © Nouwens/Shutterstock (center, right); p. 71: © National Trust Images/John Millar; p 72: © marekuliasz/Shutterstock (top); © Dn Br/Shutterstock (left); © Morphart Creation/Shutterstock (center left); © Jka/Shutterstock (bottom) © chronicler/Shutterstock (center); © WolfDrawing/Shutterstock (bottom) © shooarts/Shutterstock (right); p. 74: © Morphart Creation/Shutterstock (right); © Maryna S/Shutterstock (far left); © Liliya Shlapak/Shutterstock (left); © winnond/Shutterstock; © Nouwens/Shutterstock; p. 75: © winnond/Shutterstock; p. 76: © Alex Leo/Shutterstock (top); © mamanamsai/Shutterstock (center); pp. 76–77 © Jiraphoto/Shutterstock; p. 77: © winnond/Shutterstock; pp. 88–89: © Irina Vaneeva/Shutterstock; pp. 90–91 © Sheryl C.S. Johnson/Shutterstock; pp. 92–93: © rzarek/Shutterstock

96